C000043668

Heartbreak & Hope
poems for the healing woman

written by:

Naomi Marie

also known as

I DEDICATE THIS BOOK TO THE WOMEN WHO HAVE GONE THROUGH IT.

WHO ARE GOING THROUGH IT.

WHO ONLY KNOW HOW TO GO THROUGH IT.

WHOSE MOTHERS AND GRANDMOTHERS HAVE GONE THROUGH IT TOO.

THE WOMEN WHO WANT TO CHANGE THE FATE OF THEIR LINE.

HEALING THROUGH THE HEARTBREAK AND HOPE.

Please be warned that these poems may elicit triggers that include physical abuse, emotional abuse, religious abuse, and domestic violence.

The written works within this book are based on my own life experiences; and they include reflections of events that may trigger some readers. Please, proceed with caution.

This book is a compilation of poetry, thoughts, hopes, prayers, and raps written by Naomi Marie, *Chingona Healer* over the course of 3 years. These pages are a reflection of internal and external struggles, stories, and are witness to her healing process. Over the 3 years that these works were created, Naomi went through separation and divorce, began navigating single-motherhood. She also began dating (after 7 years of marriage) which rerrsulted in new situations and relationships with friends, family, and lovers. All the while processing and healing from trauma and subsequently treating C-PTSD. There are also works that were written during 2020 /the Covid-19 global pandemic.

These pages offer inspiration and hope to the reader. Naomi was able to overcome her circumstances and get to a place of thriving and living her best life. Naomi did not have a large or strong support system and often she struggled alone, she used writing as a way to organize and reflect her thoughts and feelings.

The people that are the subject of these written works are mostly anonymous, and names have either been omitted, changed or abbreviated, and in some cases given nicknames. These works are the product of pushing through pain, fears, rejection, solitude, and tears.

It is her hope that these works help others heal. She is rooting for everyone Black and Brown (because her feminism is intersectional). Some works in this book celebrate BIPOC experiences, Naomi identifies as a queer woman of color (Latina).

FAMILY—RELATIONSHIPS

MOTHERHOOD—RELATIONSHIPS

DATING—RELATIONSHIPS

EX—RELATIONSHIPS

RE—SITUATIONSHIPS

SELF—REFLECTION

SEXUALITY—REFLECTION

SELF—TRANSFORMATION

FUTURE—SELF

family ———

relationships

THE CYCLE

Abuse
Fear
Anxiety
Depression
Trauma
Pain

I could never make sense

of this cycle

The cycle I was born in
The cycle I grew up in
The one that almost killed me

You can't make chaos
Make sense

There's no logic
No rhyme or reason

Just pain
That nobody questioned

Because that's the way things were
I'm sure you heard that before

Tell me why
Why were they—that way?
Why am I the only one questioning?

Make it make sense

It doesn't

and it never will

Chaos is like a hurricane
A tornado, an earthquake
Leaving damage in their wake

And the cycle continues
If you just sit around and wait
For change to happen to you
Like the trauma happened to you

Change and growth
Don't just happen
They need a conscious effort

Growth comes from understanding
Change happens when deciding

to take your fate into your own hands

You have to make change happen

HOME

I've been looking for a place called home.
I never had a home to call my own.
The one I grew up in was,
a shelter full of blood-related strangers.
It was a house, not a home.
I've been looking for a place called home.
Thinking I'd have one,
with a family of my own.

K.G.Y.M.

Never trust a Pisces

with a knife

They'll stab you

in the back

or in the leg

it'll leave a scar

That shit is not normal

Stop taking out your emotions on others

R.E.M.

This isn't about the group
This is about a person
Her, she's a female
And she used to be my sister

I learned that sisters support
They show up
They need you as much as you need them
To lean on, to love, to live

She wasn't that to me
Never was
She laughed when I cried
Made me cry on purpose

A bully, my whole life
My worst critic
She thought I was her competition
That's how the patriarchy wants it
Women against women

When it comes to everything
Success, education, love, duty
The gaze of men

I just wanted a sister
Not someone who would purposely trigger me
So that she would feel better about herself
Not someone who hurt me

On purpose
Or someone who roots for you to fail
So she could be better than you in her mind

Not someone who put you down
Every chance they got
Who was worried about how others see her
Instead of looking within

Sisters?
Just because we share DNA
Doesn't mean that you deserve that title

You have a chip on your shoulder
Still,
Because what I did and what you didn't do
That wasn't my fault

You have no one to blame but yourself
You didn't take charge of your life
And I did and that's all it comes down to

Neither of us had support
Neither of us had love
From them
But I decided to dig deep and look within
And you sought it from others

Real love comes from within
You never saw the love I gave
Because your definition of love came with pain

HEALING

We are all healing from something
Wounds so deep
We can't talk about them
Wounds that we don't recognize
When someone asks us

Generational trauma
It's in our DNA
Whether we grow up with our families or not
It's in us
Who are ancestors were
Who we are now

We are connected
In our blood
In our bones
Our bodies carry it all
The effects of trauma
Compounded in the family line

For me, my DNA tells me
I come from Colonizers and the Colonized
Conquistadors and Indigenous Mexicans
From Mestizo and Enslaved people

Decades of war, and struggle
Of death and deception
Injustice in my blood

The injustice of colonization
Of slavery, of genocide
The cruelty of it all
Disgust and distrust
I was born with it all

But I'm different
It stops with me
I'm passing healing down

My son and future generations deserve better
I know this, now I know I deserved better too
But I can only course correct in the present
For the future

I have to acknowledge the past
So that I don't repeat it

SOLAMENTE

People keep telling me

I'm not alone in the world

I have a hard time believing them

Because when I'm sad and down

I'm alone

No one is there

To reach out to

To hold and comfort me

I just want a hug

To feel loved

Sometimes I think

I'll go my whole life

Without that feeling

MOTHER

There have been amazing poems and songs about
wonderful mothers, but this isn't one of those...
Because my mother wasn't wonderful.
She was human, flaws and all.
That is putting it lightly...
Maybe there was a time she cared?
Or loved me in her **TWISTED** *way?*
But I think that's my brain
Trying to make sense of it all
She used to say "I beat you because I love you"
After she hit me...
But I couldn't decide
Whether the hitting or the screaming was worse
They both **BROKE** *me down*
Throwing things when she was **ANGRY**
Raising 7 kids couldn't be easy
But that wasn't an excuse
I was abused
From all the trauma and pain
I take with me
How not to be a mother
I used to think my dad was worse
His emotional and verbal abuse
But she was **CHAOS** *when she screamed*
Lost control when she hit
Sat on me
Pulled my hair
Dragged me
Apparently
I had it the worst as the youngest?

LIFE

I was raised in a religious cult.

That shit fucked me up.

UNTITLED no. 1

Sometimes I see happy families

People having babies

Getting dogs

People whose parents are in their lives

And I get sad

Not because I'm (not) happy for them

But because **I WANT THAT** so bad

I want a family of my own

DEAR "DAD",

You were the man that was supposed to teach me how I should be loved by a man. But you never once said you loved me. You never told me I was pretty or smart or kind. Instead if I made a mistake you called me stupid. It wasn't until I got to college and used that word in casual conversation towards someone that they told me it was mean. It was an everyday occurrence in our house "stupid-idiot" we were somehow both.

I never saw you cry, though I'm told you did twice. Once when your mom died and the other time when I ran away. Only then you said I had your mothers eyes. To my face when you were yelling at me - you said I had lying eyes. You thought I did the things I was accused of.

Truth is, you didn't know how to love your kids. You were repeating the same toxic behavior that your dad did. You didn't know how to love yourself either. I went from toxic relationship to toxic relationship because I didn't know how to love myself either.

There was a time when I lived alone and I spilled milk and I yelled and screamed at myself about how "stupid and wasteful I was" and that I "need to watch what I was doing." I wrote about it then jokingly. But no it wasn't funny, that was an example of self-hate.

When I became a mother I wanted to be the parent I always needed. I swore I wouldn't make the same mistakes that mine did. I outwardly love my son. He knows it's human to cry, and he hears that I love him and I also show him.

It wasn't easy to break this cycle... but hopefully soon—he will see how his mom truly deserves to be loved. Someone is going to come into my life that is going to love me so hard, I'm going to swept off my feet. I am so excited. He's going to be loved too. Because no man can love me fully without loving my son too.

Thanks for co-signing student loans for me, but that wasn't love either - that was your own guilt for not believing me when I was telling the truth.

Sincerely,

The daughter who learned to love herself.

FAMILY FIRST

I'm trying real hard to let go of the resentment
For 8 years the world was on my shoulders

You watched from the sidelines
It just seemed like you were getting over

I waited, debated, for something to change
I kept doin' me, trying to succeed

You brought me down
Weighed on me like an anchor

I was drowning
And you kept me down

But, I got away
I'm a survivor

Now I'm just trying to do my best
For my seed who doesn't see the struggle

I like it that way
I just want to protect him

Even if that means—from you
Don't let him down like you did me

Expectations are a bitch
But you were a man that didn't keep his word

Not sure which is worse
You were supposed to put your family first

UNTITLED no. 2

I'm tired of being "there" for people
who don't reciprocate.

This breaks my heart.

BABY GIRL

Keep your head up
Protect yourself
Sometimes, runaway

Be grateful
and kind
It's okay to be sassy

Show people your brilliance
Don't hide in the corner
It's okay to get noticed

Continue to love hard
Just give love sparingly
to those who reciprocate

It's not your fault if things don't work out
that's just the way it was supposed to be

Be grateful for what was, for what is
and what will be

Don't forget to hug yourself
and love yourself
it's been a long-hard-journey to here.

WAY BACK WHEN

I wish
I could
remember the
last time
I felt loved.

When it was
unconditional
and free.

Before people
wanted things
from me
in exchange.

Before
I had to grow up
and protect myself
because
no one else
would do it.

motherhood—

— relationships

MOTHERING

*On hard days... I have to be my son's mother
and I have to mother myself.*

I'm a motherless child.

I'm a child that doesn't have a home.

That has never felt safe.

*That has to build a safe place for her own child,
when she doesn't have the experience
or the knowledge to do so.*

Everything is survival.

When will it end?

When will she be safe?

When will she be secure?

When will she be held in love and devotion?

I'm tired of being strong.

I'm tired of holding it together.

I'm tired of being every thing for myself and my son.

*I need help,
I need someone to take care of me.*

UNTITLED no. 3

I need help with my son.

I need love.

I need affection.

I need a hug.

I'm tired of hurting.

HOW I MOTHER

My baby boy, you will *always* be my baby boy.
I love you beyond the stars that we can see.

You come from me, but not from my trauma.
Just like I'm not from my parents trauma.

But they gave me that burden, on top of my own.
Just as their parents did them.

But you won't bear anyone's burdens,
Except your own.

You are of a new generation.
It stops with me.

I made that promise to you,
The day I held you in my arms for the first time.

I didn't know that when I said,
        "I'm not going to be like my parents,
                I'm doing *everything* differently."

It would mean that I'd heal
the generational trauma passed to me.

BIRTH DAY

When I held you in my arms
The day you were born
My baby boy's birthday
You were early
32 weeks
Nothing went as planned
All that mattered was you
That you were healthy
I was scared the entire time
Because I was alone
Your dad was there
But not present
And I cried each night
Until I had you
Until I held you
Your tiny fingers
And chubby cheeks
And your smile
Your dimples
And baby hair
You were so tiny
And I looked at you
I was so in love
So instantly
I promised you
that I would not let
anything that happened to me
To happen to you
And I haven't
All I want is for you
to be happy, healthy, and whole

THIS IS MY ODE: TO BLACK WOMEN.

I see you
Your pain
Your struggles

The trauma you carry
That's not even your load to bear
It's been handed down, generational

You don't deserve to struggle
or to suffer
but, please don't stop

The world needs you
Your love, devotion
Your passion

Black women birthed this Nation
Raped and forced to Breed
Their seed scattered
Because of White mens' Greed

Have you ever known a Black woman's love?
I have

She has been my teacher, my mentor, my best friend, my
lover, my family, my principal, and professors, my sister,
cousin, my Auntie, my mom… because when you're at her
house… a Black woman will take care of you, like a mom.

But with the pain they carry
So too, the dreams of a nation
But yet the nation
Vilifies, dehumanizes, victimizes
There's no justification
in the way you're treated

It is wrong
It is hateful
and in the nation of the dreamers
It doesn't belong

I am not a Black woman
but that does not mean
I cannot support her, love her
Fight for her

You cannot have her riches
So you teach yourselves to hate her

Her beauty, her power, intelligence, and grace
Her natural hair, with all the kinks and curls and kitchens

And her skin
The smoothness
The softness
and its' tone
sometimes silky brown, deep with red-tones
maybe caramel, or honey, or beautiful brown-skin.
Melaninated magic
I lose myself in its depth

Beautiful, Beautiful
Black Women
I hear you
I see you
I love you

Keep going
The nation of dreamers need you
To keep leading, teaching, loving
Learning, inventing, caring

Black Women: this is my ode, to you .

LANGSTON HUGHES

"Mother, to son"

Life for me

I tell my son

He knows

It wasn't a *crystal stair*

But I show him

I give him

The lessons

But

Not

The

Pain

So he can walk further

With knowledge

How to *avoid the nails*

The *worn floorboards*

Or when there are *none at all*

It's how I heal

It's how he heals

It's how he can go further

Live longer

Be happy

Be whole

dating ——————

—relationships

WAS IT A DREAM?

I don't know where to begin
I was all in
Not at first
You got mad and,
I wanted you to prove,
that you weren't a catfish

The lunches
The dinners
The gifts
Filling up my gas tank
Just putting money in my wallet

I didn't even know how to react to this
Such care and kindness
I never spent a dime with you
And you looked at me like I was,
the only one in the room

You really broke my heart
It took me awhile to move on
I would have gone with you anywhere
I just wanted to be with you

It wasn't about any of the material things
It was the way you looked at me, and held me,
You took pictures of me from across the room
I was falling in love with you

But maybe it was all a dream
That came crashing down
The day that you lost your dad
I didn't hear from you for awhile

Reality was, that you'd have to return home
To ▮▮▮▮▮ and you said I couldn't come
You said it was no place for me
And no place to raise a son

What would I do there?
The only thing I wanted to do was
To be with you
So simple

But you knew what you had to do
Duty before dreams
Mother and siblings before me
You ended it

I've tried to find that same feeling
The one I had with you
Easy and warm
Simple and sweet
But it escapes me
It feels like it was just a dream

MY LOVE

I didn't see **YOU** coming
But **YOU'VE** entered my life
And now that **YOU'RE** here
YOU got me thinking twice

I don't know how **YOU** do it
But **YOU** feed my soul
The way **YOU** look at me
How **YOU** listen and exchange

When I'm near **YOU**
I feel balance, joy, hope, and peace
All good things
And there is no time

YOU are special to me
I feel it deep inside myself
I'm not wanting… not searching…
My soul is stirring, fulfilled from within

We are two whole souls
That compliment, not complete
A yin and yang
Mingling and meeting in the middle

When I think of **YOU**
I feel warm
I get excited to see **YOU**
I feel **YOUR** love

When we touch, it's electric
Every sense of self… tingling
YOU pull me in
And I am drawn to you like a magnet
The kisses are soft and direct

The way we connect
After an intellectual or emotional exchange
The physical pursues
YOU know where to touch me
How to hold me
How to comfort me
How to please me

We are intertwined
Being near **YOU**, feels like home
Safe, supported, understood, and seen
It just feels like everything

YOU have me believing in soul-mates
Because I think I've reached a higher level
I have nothing to offer **YOU** but myself
And it finally feels like enough

All I want…
Is **YOU**
I belong with **YOU**

THANKS TO YOU

I finally know what it feels like

to be in love, to be loved, to feel safe and secure.

our attachment is healthy, wholesome,

spiritual, physical, intellectual, emotional.

It was a story that was meant to be.

It could never work with anyone else,

because there's only one **YOU**.

We have been making our way to each other,

since we entered this life from the last

YOU make me laugh, **YOU'RE** so funny

I'm my whole-self with **YOU**

I get to be me, just me

Not just a mom, or an entrepreneur or board member

or any other titles I've had in my life

nothing else matters, with you in my life

There is no time and the limit does not exist

intertwined and wrapped up into each other

infinity

connected on a soul level, cosmic, destined, natural

hold my hand, because **YOUR** touch

gives me fuel, to keep going

A POEM FOR YOU

I miss **YOU**,
>*when we're not together.*

I love **YOU**,
>*all the time.*

I think about **YOU**,
>*when I masturbate.*

We laugh,
>*and sometimes I cry.*

The way **YOU** make me feel
I might be able to describe it:
>*calm,*
>*safe,*
>*loved,*
>*warm,*
>*full,*
>*happy,*
>*at home,*
>*silly,*
>*hopeful,*
>*passionate,*
>*taken care of...*

And I know, that,
>*there is no one else like **YOU.***

I HATE YOU

I hate **YOU**–so much, just because I love **YOU.**

I hate that, I can't get mad at **YOU.**

I hate that I love, **YOUR** stupid face.

And I hate the way, I miss **YOU** when we aren't together.

I hate that **YOU** make me so happy,

I literally could not live without **YOU.**

And I hate that, I need **YOU.**

I hate that, **YOU** make me cry just because I didn't hear from **YOU.**

YOU make me laugh so hard, so much that,

I think that I could die with how much my sides hurt.

I hate that **YOU** make me wait, and I'm learning how to be patient and shit.

I fucking hate how **YOUR** smile makes me smile.

I hate that sex with **YOU** is so damn perfect.

And the way **YOU** know exactly what I want,

without me ever saying anything.

And I hate that **YOU'RE** the first person,

to really care for and take care of me.

I hate that, I don't even know, just exactly

how much **YOU** love me,

because I have never experienced love like this before.

No one has ever, loved me like **YOU.**

I hate that it took me too long to find **YOU.**

I hate that I pushed **YOU** away, then I ran away.

And then **YOU** took me back, and I didn't even really have to ask.

I hate that **YOU** are so into me, but **YOU** are just way too cool to verbally express it.

So, I swallow my pride because I notice it, in all the things **YOU** do for me.

I hate that **YOU** are my ideal match.

And to me, **YOU** are perfect.

YOU are everything I want in a partner.

YOU'RE such a fucking jerk-face!

I love **YOU.**

INTOXICATED

somewhere, between feeling like i'm high on **YOU**

and the withdrawal i have without **YOU**

i'm crying

because i just want **YOU** near me

but **YOU** require space

i want **YOU** and **YOU** want me

but we, don't want the same things

is the taste good enough to sustain?

no, because i constantly need a fix

i get high on how **YOU** make me feel

how **YOU** make me laugh

the way **YOU** make me smile

but **YOU** also make me sad

i cry

YOU make me happy

i cry

YOUR kisses linger

YOUR touch shocks the life in me

and the way **YOU** love me

passionate

intense

visceral

i'm trying to figure out

if i can live without **YOU**

no one makes me feel like this

but the way i want **YOU**

i want you like i need air

like i need **YOU** in my life

YOU make me feel alive

and once you leave

i miss **YOU**

and it fucking hurts like hell

ECSTASY & JOY

YOU fill me up
YOUR presence
YOUR warm embrace
The way **YOU** make me laugh
When I hear **YOUR** voice
When **YOU** hold my hand
The way **YOU** look at me

It's how **YOU** make me feel
Just by being **YOU**
It's how **YOU** love me
For just being me

This acceptance
This love
YOUR love for me
Makes me overjoyed
Whole
Grounded
Alive

AND SHOW OUT

I didn't even know that...
 I receive love
  and show love
   differently,
    *until **YOU** came into my life.*

*It's how **YOU** show up for me.*

***YOU** have my back*
 when I need it.

***YOU** comfort*
 and care for me
  and that does it for me.

*All I need is **YOU**.*
 I want your love,
  no one else's.

REDACTED RESIGNATION

███████████

To: Human Resources &
████████████████████████
████████████████████

Dear ████████████████████████

Thank you for the opportunity to work for
you, ████████████████████████████████████
██████████ However, I can't in good faith continue my
employment with ████████████████████████
██████████ This position has negatively affected my
mental health for too long. And no job or amount of
money is worth my peace and mental health. This is my
letter of resignation, effective immediately.

Sincerely,
Naomi ████████████

TRIGGERED BY ASSOCIATION

I've never felt so verbally attacked before.

(not even by K.M.)

I don't know, if—*IT* was a sense of entitlement?

or maybe... she was—feeling protective?

But, whatever *IT*—was,

IT—did not leave a good feeling with me!

Maybe, *IT'S*—not something that she would—do?

and maybe—she's feeling a sense of ownership?

Maybe, she—thinks she's—better than me?

I don't know, what *IT*—is?

Maybe she—is insecure?

IT'S—frustrating, whatever *IT* is, or was,

just because, I don't like confrontation.

IT triggered me.

FEELS

I have loved **YOU**
Before I knew **YOU**
I am certain of this

No one else matters
Past, present, future
Just **YOU**

YOU fill my thoughts
And my heart
I feel our connection
In my soul

It feels like
I just met my soulmate
YOU are my person
Undoubtedly

I want **YOU**
I need **YOU**
I feel **YOU**

Every day I spend with **YOU**
Feels like time does not exist
Hours take longer and slower to pass

Being in **YOUR** arms
Is a safe place
And a home that I've been searching for
But only have in **YOU**

It feels like
I've known **YOU** my whole life
Instead I just met **YOU**

In one night I felt closer to **YOU**
Than someone I spent a decade with
I never want to go a day
Without **YOU** in my life

YOU are my love and my peace
My home and my forever
My protector and my cheerleader
My soulmate and the love of my life

YOU are my person
And I loved you before
I knew **YOU** (in this life)

Our souls are forever linked
And I will always find my way to **YOU**
I am certain

HAVE YOU EVER...?

Remembered a day so clearly,
that you could,
paint a picture,
from your memory?

What about feeling,
that time passed too quickly,
while every second lingered to pass?

Been so comfortable,
and at peace in someone's presence,
they just felt like an extension of you?

A day that was natural, free, and fun.

The joy I felt that day with you,
was how I want to feel for the rest of my life.

Full of all the feelings, full of hope and joy.

Take my hand,
I think we can.

BABE

YOU are everything

Everything I've been wanting

Needing... craving...

YOU, my sweetheart

My reflection

I want to know everything about **YOU**

I want to love all of **YOU**

With all of me

I want **YOU** forever

I am **YOURS** in this life

And the next

I will continue to find **YOU**

I'm ready to give you everything

everything **YOU** want and need

I want to hold onto **YOU**

I want to make **YOU** so happy

Give **YOU** the love **YOU** deserve

The love **YOU** want and need

Devote my time to **YOU**

I can't wait to marry **YOU**

Travel the world

Take care of **YOU**

Learn all your favorite things

Love on **YOU** every chance I get

HÁBLAME

Tell me about **YOUR** dreams

YOUR hopes and fears

Tell me

THE WAY YOU MAKE ME FEEL

The way **YOU** hold me
The way **YOU** make me feel
YOUR tender touch
YOUR soft lips
The kisses on my forehead
How **YOU** rub my head

Then it's my turn to hold **YOU**
Be **YOUR** peace
YOUR comfort and safe space
YOUR head in my neck and chest
Allowing **YOU** to rest
Allowing **YOU** to be soft and vulnerable

YOU, are the one I need and want
I want to be next to **YOU,** always
YOU, are my safe place, my protector
My partner, and my home
I can't wait to be your family
And wake up next to **YOU** every day
Share our life and love always

Maybe one day we'll say I do
Join in marriage and name
The way we hold hands and rub fingers
Gentle and warm forever in love

HACE FRIO

I just want **YOU** next to me

Keeping me warm and safe

DÁMELO

Someone to dance with

Act silly and laugh

Make funny faces with me

Be my joy and my peace

Explore and have adventures with

Grow and learn with

BE MY OTTER

I love **YOU**
YOU make me feel safe
I don't have a guard when I'm with **YOU**
Could **YOU** be my soulmate?
I've been waiting my whole life to meet **YOU**
I'm ready for forever
But maybe we aren't going to be together?
If not, I wish **YOU** the best
I want **YOU** to have all **YOUR** desires and wants in life
But selfishly, I just want to be with **YOU**
The way **YOU** look at me the way **YOU** kiss me
YOUR gentle touch and sweet words
I know **YOU** felt it too
Our connection is so electric and so deep
YOU sweep me off my feet
I've never felt as safe as I do, in **YOUR** arms
I feel free with **YOU**
YOU are my match, my equal, and my partner
YOU show me love I have not felt in this life
I need **YOU** by my side
Just to walk together through life
I'm here to support **YOU** and be **YOUR** rock
I'm here to see **YOUR** soft side
Tell me **YOU** feel it too
Tell me **YOU** want this too
I want to grow with **YOU**
Hand in hand
Just like sleeping otters

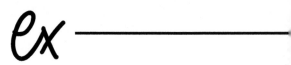

—relationships

LIFE IS A BITCH

Life is a bitch
Anytime you think you're ahead
She bitch slap you

Take two steps forward
And something happens
That sets you way back
It'll take you
Two years to come back from

It's hard to stay positive
When you got people
Bringing you down
Kicking you
While you're on the floor

People who say they love you
Then they're slapping you
With papers
Telling you you're a walrus

AKA fat
Last week
You said more of me to love
But love don't live here no more

Winters cold
Not colder than your heart
Hielo
Say hello to the door that
Smacked you in the face

I got news to share
But no one to share it with
You were the one
I chose to share my life with

That don't mean nothing
You're holding moving against me
But it was your idea
I never asked you for nothing
You have no idea

If I would have known
You were gonna resent me
For something you wanted to do
I would have divorced you
A long time ago
And never let you come back

You told me to guard my heart
With people
But you were the one
I should've guarded it from

OVER IT

I'm over it

I'm over you

I can't

Don't try

It won't work

Done

DATING A NARCISSIST

I've been hurt enough
Don't hurt me too
I really like you
But I'm so confused

I don't know what you want
One day I get all your attention
The next I'm left wondering if you got my text
Do you just want sex?

Are you ready for what I want
I thought we were on the same page
But you aren't really checking for me
And trying to not catch feelings

I feel so defeated
Not sure what you want
Or if you even like me
I just need honesty and consistency

I don't think that's too much to ask for
The bar is kinda low
So I'm not gonna settle for less than that
Anymore would be a disregard for all of me

I AM A RUNNER

You were everything I wanted in a partner

But I got the best of me again

I pushed you away, I'm good at that

I put so many expectations on you

And I wanted you to prove me wrong

I was wrong, but not how I expected to be

You were everything you said and you showed me

But I didn't believe it

I wanted you to be like every other guy

But you weren't, and I didn't want to accept it

I only know trauma, abuse, and pain

You offered something else

Something I wanted

But it was new, different, and scary

I didn't know what to do

So I ran, so fast

I'm sure you didn't see that coming

You could have anyone you want

And you picked me

But I didn't know how to accept you

You wanted me, you saw me

But I didn't believe you

ONE-SIDED

Lopsided
Unequal
Non-reciprocal
Conversations on read
Words left unsaid

One effort
One-sided
Hanging out to dry
Let me be free
Let me fly

I'm held back
By these one-sided conversations
The text threads
Are just me
Talking to myself
Wishing you'd reply

This isn't what I signed up for
You said you'd do better
But different day
Same old shit

I'm tired of these games
So over this same thing
If I wanted to talk to myself
I would
I don't need you for that

This isn't an exchange
This is one-sided
I'm tired of trying

I'm the one giving
My time
My attention
My energy
This ain't it

Reciprocal or nothing
I'm not doing this again
I had 8 years of this

Can't take this
This is pain
This hurts
Trauma trigger
Panic, pressure, stress
Can't breathe
With this tightness in my chest
All from this one-sided conversation

The lack of communication
Lack of care
Lack of concern
Lack of love
Lack of consistency
All from this one-sided conversation

LOVE HURTS

It hurts me that, you don't want to try

It hurts that, I know—you love me

It hurts that I want you, and you know it

There's too much hurt

Maybe space will heal me

Maybe space, will allow for someone new

You were there for me

I feel like I need you

You just don't see it

I wish I didn't too

GAMES

I want to hate you, but I don't.
I'm actually,
mad and disappointed.

You built up a lot,
just to let me down.
You hurt me.
You didn't treat me like,
you didn't want to lose me.

In the end, you're too young,
and just playing games.

I have no time for bullshit
or games.
There's the door,
love don't live here no-mo'.

YOU, AGAIN

I can't get **YOU** off my mind
I'm the one who said goodbye
I pushed **YOU** away

We don't communicate the same
So to me, it felt like a game
Up and down
I was on a roller coaster
When I just wanted easy

It wouldn't be easy with **YOU**
And I know that I'm past struggle
I don't want to know hurt and pain again

I know if I let myself
I could love **YOU**
Forever

I think we had something
The making of a love story
It could be a fairy tale

YOU, the knight in shining armor
Me, needing to be rescued
Love at first sight

The click
Everything **YOU** wanted
Was what I wanted

I just wanted to reach out
And touch **YOU**
Through the phone

I wanted to be in **YOUR** arms
Kiss **YOUR** lips
And feel **YOUR** hands all over me

But I don't know how to be loved
And I can't communicate,
If only half my messages go answered
I wanted to be **YOUR** everything
And maybe that's where I went wrong
We started off so strong

Maybe too much
Then too little
Because, the spark fizzled

I know, if I saw **YOU**
Standing there
I'd throw caution to the wind
I would leap, before I looked
And with every ounce of me
Pray, **YOU'D** catch me

But, if **YOU** didn't
I'd know, it wasn't real
I don't even know how I'd feel

But maybe **YOU** were mine?
In another lifetime?
Maybe we could be lovers again?
In the next life
Or maybe this really is the end?

DREAMS, DEFERRED

I'm not insecure
I am ready for you
I'm ready for this
I'm ready for forever
I won't let the distance
Or your job get to me
Everything you are is
Everything I want

This feels different than
Other guys and other times
I feel connected and
My heart longs to be near you
I feel your calmness
I feel safe and secure in your arms

I can't wait to give you a baby
A baby made from love
A family made whole
I have so much love to give
I can't wait to give it to you
I want your lips
I need your kisses
And hugs and cuddles
I want forever right now

But I need to be patient
Real things take time

YOU WANTED A PIECE OF ME

You saw me, fully
But had other priorities

Mixed messages, and confusion
No lies, but twisted half-truths

You weren't open
You shut-down
So, I shut you out
And I don't regret that

But, you need to know
You are missing me
The best thing,
that ever could be

I just wanted you
In any way you could allow
But you only wanted a piece
And I know that now

Stick to the version,
of me in your head
Do us both a favor,
the flame is dead

DIS & DISMISS

Get out my face, Boy
Get of my space, Boy

Away from my place, now
You're wasting my time, how?

You were a distraction
Such a beautiful distraction

Played games with my heart
I told you stop, told you stop

I'm worse off with you
Better off without you

You not holding me down
You're holding me back
Setting me back
Can't get my time back

Cost me money
Eat my food
Don't buy me shit

I thought you were different
But you're more of the same
Kept playin' games
I'm done with you

Chewed me up
And spit me out too
What did I do to you?

I gave you my heart
You tossed it aside

Only care about yourself
Like a fucking child
But, you were beautiful

Just a distraction that,
Told me what I wanted to hear
I just wanted you near

I don't need a distraction
I need a man
Someone to hold my hand
It's over, you're over

Boy… bye

¡ADIOS!

Sometimes, you have to leave.
Sometimes, they have to miss you.
Sometimes, they don't appreciate you.
Sometimes, they don't love you.

Give me some space.
Get out of my face.
I hate to do this,
Because, I think I love you.

But, we don't want the same things.
So, I can't even look at you.
This hurts me as much,
(Or maybe even more?)
Than it hurts you.

A BETTER ME WITHOUT YOU

You want to talk about
How you doin'?

You want to talk about
What I'm doin'?

What do you want?
A pat on the back?
A high five?

7 years I waited for you
To get your shit together
To quit that shit

Now that you did, you want to drop me
Been staying right, so what you gone do?
Leave me for a white girl?

Sorry not sorry, but
I've never been a gold digger

Never had nothing or nobody
Never asked for nothing
Expected nothing from nobody

You're not the exception
You're the fucking norm

I got here because I survived
When no one had by back

I climbed out of the lion's den
With nothing but the grit of my teeth
And the scars on my body and in my heart

You talk about could have left me a long time ago?
Didn't I kick you out a while ago?
Didn't you beg me for another chance?

I remember you said I was your everything…
You said all you needed was me…

I said I needed you to man up, stand up,
Be the man I knew you, had in you

Live up to your potential baby
Don't waste all that potential baby

You let a cloud of smoke lose your way to me
Now you telling me that you can see clearly

But what you don't realize is that, I've been holding us down
And it's been weighing on me
All I needed was a little bit help
And now think you can do better than me

But what you don't realize is
I won't do bad by myself
But I can be a better me
Without you

You see, I ain't been loyal to nothing
Except you and me

And when I tell you it's a slap in the face
All I mean is that I want you there with me

I'm not going to hold your hand and pat your back
How many times have you said "You only got one son?"

Encouragement comes from the fuel of your passion inside
So how am I bringing you down when I've been nothing but on your side?

I find it frustrating that you, do what you tell me not to
You're bringing up the past, I thought you moved on too?

I said move on, I mean on to the next one...
Let's not repeat the past, let's do better for the next one

What am I supposed to do? You gave me ultimatums
And it feels like you're ready to move on to the next someone

Not wanting to spend time? Holidays?
I thought we shared something new
I thought I showed you something new

I've been listening to you
I thought I showed you
I thought we shared something

It feels like, you think, I'm holding you back
I'm next to you
Not standing in your way
It hurts that, I don't think you see it my way

FAKE FRIEND

A fake friend hates you on the low
Same person spreading rumors
But in your face is like idk

Taking you for everything you got
Then Turns around and acts like a victim
They will twist your words

And say that your actions are anything but your intent
A fake friend doesn't know how to love themselves
So they look for reasons and find fault in the love you give

The way they stab you in the heart is worse than a lover
You showed them who you were
And they exploited you, used you, abused you

They took from you
until you had nothing left for yourself
and then they called you a narcissist

They Said your love was love bombs
Then pretended not to know what any of that meant

They claim to be many things
But it's all a shiny veneer

Covered in glitter glue so you can't see the cracks
And the funny thing is they think they are fooling you

They show you
who they are
time and time again

They show you that they are a fake friend
They will talk shit to their new best friend
Because they keep making old best friends

Most of us fall for this ruse
The shiny glittery person
The outside looks so promising

But the inside is hallow and hidden
And even they don't know who they are
They keep pretending while the world passes them by

They're stuck and bitter
And you can't help them
Because they refuse to help themselves

They dispose of people like trash
They think they are right all the time
But they can't see what's in their face

Because you're their best friend
and you're giving them your best
But they can't handle it
and don't know what to do with it

So you constantly get their worst
That's why they aren't your friend
They are just there to receive

All your love, time, and energy
Constantly picking them up off the floor

But also saying you put them there and dragged them
When you were just trying to get out the door

It was all well and good
when you let them take

But once you put a stop to it
That's when you see that they are fake

All because
they can't reciprocate

—situationships

CLOSER

Come closer baby x2
I need you, I want you

Why do we do this
to each other honey

Ooo you're sweet like honey
The way you love on me

I just want you close to me
But I need to focus on me

Why do we hurt each other
When we got so much love for the other

Can't get you outta my mind
But you have no respect for time

I'm bad at communicating
And I assume way too much

But I can't live without your touch
I'm just standing here waiting on you - ooo ooo

UNTITLED no. 4

I let my guard down with you.

I thought you were different.

I guess, you were.

It hurt even more,
when you rejected me,
the second time.

HARVARD GRAD

You were a tinder match
I checked your LinkedIn *(accidentally, I swear!)*
But it matched up
We met up
For lunch, super classy

Best Thai food ever
You fed my body
My soul, and my mind
Probably the greatest
Conversation
I've ever had
With a man

You met me where I was
I didn't have dumb myself down
Or explain things to you
And honestly
It had nothing to do with Harvard
I am so much smarter than you
Well let's just say we're smart at different things

I never had someone
Make love to my thoughts
Buts that what it was
A titillating exchange of ideas
Experience, life, love, longing

Deeper than that
I could look at you
And you knew what I was thinking
The way you held me
And kissed me
Time stopped

You were late for a meeting
But you made it on time
But the thoughts and the kisses
Mingled with lingering feelings
Intrigued, entranced…
Wanting to get lost in the place
We created with our minds

And just like that
It was over
In an instant
Faster than it began
I'll forever wonder
Where we could have went
If only it could have been
Longer than lingering a moment

A FIRST KISS

The tension between conversation
Staring into each other's eyes
Biting or licking your lips
Pushing my hair out of my face
The magnetism between our bodies
Our hands touching
Our faces moving closer
Being pulled into the other
Finally our lips locking
The softness
Slightly wet, relief
Your hand rubbing me
Caressing my neck
Playing with my hair
My hand in your beard
The other one on your back
Wrapped into each other
It feels like so much more
Than our first kiss
It feels like my last first kiss

THE HARD PART

I love hard

I don't know how to do it

Any other way

I fall easy

My heart is on my sleeve

Searching for forever

FOR THE BIRDS

I'm so tired of putting myself out there to get nothing.

I know I'm great.

When am I going to find my person?

Where are they?

I can't keep doing this.

Getting hurt.

Being vulnerable.

Having hope.

Not expecting but wanting.

Am I going to be a mom again?

A wife?

Is someone going to love every bit of me?

I'm losing hope with every day.

It's just becoming hurtful.

I attract people who are not emotionally available.

They have someone that they decide they love...

or they have to move away...

or they don't want a relationship...

or they are having babies with someone else...

I'm really tired of this bullshit.

Dating is for the birds.

EXPERIENCE

I've said these words, more times than I can count.

"I don't see this going anywhere."

"You aren't giving me what I need."

"We have different communication styles."

Or simply,

Just ghosting and blocking.

Truth is,

I don't know how to love.

But worse,

I don't know how to let myself be loved.

FIRST DATE

You picked me up
Opened the door for me
You always close it too
We waited in line
For a table
I instinctively grabbed your hand
Your hands felt warm
Dry, smooth
Not soft or rough
Perfectly balanced
But standing next to you
Holding hands
And there it was
The magnetism
I leaned into it
I let myself be drawn in
Side by side
Fingers and arms intertwined
My face pressed against your arm
And I just met you
But I knew in that moment
You were special
You didn't pull away

You didn't push
You weren't surprised or startled
You remained calm
Stayed strong
Allowed me to lean on you
You didn't say anything
But you squeezed my hand a bit
tighter
To let me know, that you knew
That you felt the connection too
And then I looked up at you
You were staring straight ahead
Unflinching and unbothered
A stillness
Like a calm lake
Basking in the golden hour
Then we were seated
Next to each other
But we turned our attention
To each other's faces
We talked and joked and laughed
But it wasn't like a first date
But more like our 100th

We just fit together
The smell of ramen
A little spot in Koreatown
Not too far from my apartment
I learned you don't like mushrooms
We talked about music and art
Civil rights and dreams
Took a drive
Trying to find a place to
continue talking
It was one hell of a conversation
Dusk was fading and i mentioned
I was afraid of coyotes
You said "do you trust me?"
Instinctively I said "yes"
No hesitation
Never in my life
Have I
Trusted someone
As fast as I trusted you
You grabbed my hand
And helped me out of the car
You said with conviction

"I got you."
And I knew you truly did
We eventually made our way
To the balcony of my apartment
Where we held hands
Kissed
Pressed our heads together
Hugged
Leaned in
And tuned out
It was just us
We talked late into the night
Deleted dating profiles
Because we both knew
This was it
We had found each other
We said goodbye
And made plans for the next day
And the day after that
And so on for a week straight

PILLOW

You keep me warm
You are supportive
And comforting
I hold on to you at night
I rest my head on you
When I'm sad I cry onto you
You're always there for me
But you are lifeless
And you can't hug me back
You can't speak to me
But you are all I have right now
Feeling so alone
I need something to hold
So I squeeze you
And I wish I could breathe life into you
I wish you weren't a pillow

BASKETBALL COACH

Let's be clear, *I never met you.*
You approached me twice.
>   *It goes down in the DM's?*
You wanted to meet me in a parking garage.
Gross dude, you have issues.

You wanted a *living doll.*
Not a person.
Twisted-sick-dude.
Pretty sure you had a girlfriend.

You'd randomly delete me as a friend.
Multiple times. Make up your mind.
What are you hiding?
I'm tired of this bullshit.
I just blocked you, in the end.

18 YEARS

That's how long

You've been on my mind

In every relationship

Everywhere I go

Like *Frida's*

"Diego on my mind"

That is how I think

of you

Wanting

and wishing

Every lip was yours

and it was your hands

Tracing every curve

of my body

Feeling electrified

Wanted

Desired

Deeply

Reciprocal

A reflection of me

You

Papi

YO QUIERO

Why me?
Why not, me?
I deserve love
To be held
Kissed on the forehead
My hair swept out of my face
My face held in someone's hands
Hugged and loved
So why does love elude me?
Where's the person who can't live without me?
Who I can't live without?
Where's my love?
More than my heart feels broken
Lonely and empty
I just want to be loved
I don't want to be jealous or resentful
But when is it my turn?
Where's my person?
Waiting is painful

OFFICER GHOST

You sold me the dream
We'll buy a house
Have a baby
We'll be step-parents to each other's kids
But the truth is
You already had that
With someone else
And I'm not the first one
You sold that story too

Fancy hotels
Delicious meals
FaceTiming me during the day
Driving across the state to see me
Saying my bed was ours
Missing the vibe of my house
Saying you miss me
Holding me the entire night

Things didn't always add up
But, your job?
That was always an excuse
It's why you left me at the hotel
Why you would flee in the morning
Why you were so tired

But really
How many women were there?
It's disgusting to think about
How you treat women
To find out all of it was a lie
Just a way for you to manipulate

I could never have a baby with you
I'm so glad that she called me
I'm so glad I know the truth
Always disappearing, saying it's your job
Officer Ghost
You're just another narcissist
Lying to get what you want

I could easily be vindictive
I could lie
I could manipulate
I could be disgusting and use people
Then toss them aside
That's the difference between me and you
I chose not to

Until
I showed you
I could do it too

REJECTION

I never felt it like this

I poured out my soul to you

I gave you my heart on a platter

And your words of rejection

Cut it into pieces and you set it on fire

You turned cold

Because you reject yourself

Commitment issues

Trust issues

Emotions don't come easy to you

I was never burnt

The way you set my heart aflame

With 2 texts you crushed me

I was so exposed

Completely open

You said you were open

But I think you want to be

You aren't vulnerable or faithful

Now I'll never think of you the same

I saw how mean and ugly you are

On the inside

You take it all from me

And I'm left with nothing

You don't give because of

What they did to you

But karma-karma-karma

Always comes back around

Treating me how they did you

It won't attract abundance

Keep living in lack because you don't give love freely

FOOTBALL COACH

What can I say?
You were charming and cute
You said you liked the conversation
You were interested too

Little did I know
You'd just blow me off
Once you got what you want
You weren't interested in me

You were just *about that thing*
All work all day
Squeeze me in your schedule
Just worried about getting yours

Tossed aside
I didn't even get off
Realized you were all talk
And a misogynist at that
I guess you did me a favor

FRIEND ZONE

The greatest unrequited love song
I sing it to you
It's for you
And about you

It pains me
To see you
Go on dates
When you

Tell me about the trysts
The pleasure
How much they love you
And want you
Your desire

As much as I want you to be happy
I'd love it if you were happy with me

No one
would ever treat you how I would
I'd bring you joy,
pleasure, and happiness
Daily,
every minute and second of the day

But this is
An unrequited love song
Best friend but friend zoned

I told you how much I want you
That I love you more than a friend
I'd give you the world

But you want a husband
Not a wife
You want a man, masculine and strong

Not a woman who would be
Gentle with you,
kind and thoughtful
And generous

I'd give you the world
Because you deserve it
Because I want you to
Have everything you want

Even if it's not me

ALL TALK

Too good to be true
I didn't want it to be
I wanted to believe you
You said "I want you"
In all caps
In all seriousness
Just be my *girlfriend*
But here I am crying
Tears wetting my face
Feeling uncomfortable in my own space
I let you get a taste
You were so direct and honest
And you wanted me?
I must have been
Just the flavor of the week?
Because now I'm waiting
With my phone in my hand
But no texts, no calls, nothing
With nothing
You told me everything I need to know
As much as you want me…
You can't make space for me
I keep looking for a message
Maybe a missed call?
A hopeful fool
I really want you to be
Everything I thought you were
I wanted to be in your arms forever
But I'll probably never hear from you again

"YOUNG"

One of my oldest friends
Confessing your love
But only wanting sex
Nothing else

You'd tell me your fears
Your hopes and dreams
But you don't want to be in love
No labels

Just when it's convenient
I used to be able to call you
When I couldn't sleep
When I needed help
In an emergency

Now we're strangers
We don't speak
You hurt me
Wanted to pour onto me emotionally
Fulfill you sexually
But didn't want me romantically

So I made the decision
To leave you where you're at
You couldn't meet me in the middle
Because you didn't want all of me

r/NICEGUY

You said you loved me
But you weren't honest with me
I thought we could talk about anything
But apparently I'm a *"drain"*
"I drain you emotionally"
"I only talk about me"
You would *"never date me"*
I'm *"too much"*
I'm *"triggery and dependent"*

But you didn't have healthy boundaries
When it came to me
That's not my fault

It was all messy and confusing
and I loved you too
and I wanted to date you
and wanted to do for you

I always wanted to date you
You didn't want me in college either
Except you'd show up at my door
Night after night
and I would hold you and you held me
Sometimes we'd just sleep
It hurt me then
that you didn't want to date me
and it hurts me even more now
Because I thought that
You—saying you loved me
And that—I meant a lot to you

Because I was
"The most consistent thing in your life..."
Like maybe you felt the same way?

But you didn't
and you didn't want to hurt me
so you didn't tell me the truth
You let me go on with my feelings
you continued to let me in
and drain you
and force you to talk about things
that you didn't want to talk about

But how can I force you?
To do something against your will?
We were on the phone
I didn't threaten you
or hold you captive
or manipulate you

We talked about everything
Things that were uncomfortable
secrets, life
hopes, dreams
Apparently, I'm a *bad friend?*
According to you

Because I wanted more
You didn't tell me that
You didn't want to date me *(in particular)*

Just that–you didn't want to date
You weren't clear with me
The lines were blurred

You said you didn't want to hurt me
I got hurt though
Too many times–by you
Did you think that you left the door open?
That possibly–you lead me on?

If you had told me the truth
I would have left you alone
a long time ago
you could've had your peace
and I could have my heart intact

I'm not the version of me in your head
Some victim, damsel in distress
Desperate for a relationship

I don't want to date just anyone
I want something real
Excuse me–I thought that
being friends with you
could potentially grow into something more
But I never pushed it on you

Yeah, I asked why we weren't dating
That was your chance, to be honest
but you were a coward
you let me do the dirty work
you made me exit

You said you cared about me?
I think you cared more about–
"Not being a bad guy"
Oh no, are you a *nice guy?*
The kind Reddit threads are written about?

I wish that–I never found out
that you were an asshole
I wish that–the college version of you
was still in my head
And maybe?
That we never even met
I wish–I wasn't there for you
when you needed me
Because you made me feel like shit
for thinking you'd be there for me
when I needed you, too

GASLIT & PROJECTING

Sometimes I think about how someone as loving and handsome as you, could like me? You call me beautiful, gorgeous, and sexy... and sometimes I don't believe you. Not because of anything to do with you. It's only because I was abused for so long, and called names like walrus... and for about 8 years felt unloved, and undesirable. I carry that trauma and rejection in me and am constantly fighting the negative thoughts in my head. I've been used so much, I don't remember the last time someone just wanted to be next to me. But you, I can't get you out of my head. Your tender touch and sweet kisses on my head and forehead. Me? The best sexual experience you've ever had? Really? Yes, really... You really looked like you could explode. The way you held on to me, kissing and licking me so full of passion and desire. You brought me to another level. How can I deny how you treat me? A man of little words, it's hard to know what you're thinking. But the way you look at me, the way you rub my head, fingers, and back... I feel it. The way you buried your head in my chest like I was your safe space. I want that every day. Because you are mine. I feel at ease and at peace with you and I want that forever. In this lifetime and all of the ones that come next.

"CHEF"

I'm still confused
You said you wanted to be *exclusive*
But didn't want to delete your tinder profile?

Was it about clout?
Are you insecure?
Just tryin' to bag this hottie?

Introducing me to cousins
Saying we look good together
But why wouldn't you delete your tinder?

Let's talk about matches
Maybe you had a few
and that was a confidence boost
But I had over 300*
and was willing to delete mine for you

A word of advice, go easy on the salt

*At the time, in a small city in Michigan

UNTITLED no. 5

More than like

Need you

Want you

Crave you

Respect you

Understand you

Obsessed with you

Desire you

Undeniable

Attracted

Irresistible

THE ONE YOU MARRY*

I'm not a backup
or a side piece
Nor do I want to be in a situationship

You either want me or you don't
There's no gray area when it comes to my heart

I want to be with someone(s)
who chooses me
and is proud to have me
I don't want to be hidden or ignored

I am a prize
I'm more precious than gold
I'm more than beautiful
more than sexy
I'm smart, and warm, loving, understanding
and I want to grow with someone

I'm a mother-fucking catch
Where is my someone(s)?
I want to be held and feel their love

*Marry, as in an acknowledged agreement of commitment. It
could include an agreed upon duration of time, and does not
have to be a government-legally-recognized marriage.

TWIN-FLAME

I've never met you before
But somehow I know you
So easy to talk to
So easy to laugh with
Hours on the phone and texting all day
I knew I couldn't stay away

It's been a really weird year
But you were pretty constant
I fucked up, and I pushed you away
I lied, I ghosted and I'm sorry

You did the same thing to me
And it wasn't revenge
I didn't try to get back at you
But now I understand

We are two of the same
My reflection staring back at me
We have the same wants, needs, and fears

We both pushed away, ran away
Hurt the other, lied, ghosted, self-sabotaged
We don't trust or believe
            others to keep their word
We're so fucking jaded
            because we've been so hurt

It's hard to let someone in
            and tear down the walls
It's hard to believe
            that someone will be there
And be what we've been waiting for
Our entire lives
We're standing right there

We've never met though
But I know how you love
It's hard, because I'm the fucking same
Fall hard, fall deep, it's your entire existence
I see that in you, a reflection of me

You want that forever
Soul-joining, life-bond, that deep
            everything
One person to be your entire world
I know because I want that too

That's why we do the things we do
Because what we want is so elusive
So crazy, so not normal
People are scared of it
They can't embrace it like we do
We know it exists
We feel it
And I know because I see that in you
You are my reflection

GHOSTED

We talked every day

For two weeks straight

Then the day before our date

Silence.

Nothing.

Did you die?

Like WTF?

No text

No phone call

I tried to comprehend

Couldn't make sense of it

I called and texted

Felt like an idiot

It all felt reciprocal

But you ended up being typical

Thought you were my person

But you ghosted me

TEXTING

On read
Seen
Wtf does that mean?

Why can't you reply?
I feel ignored
I feel rejected

I know it's just not me
But, it's kind of triggering
This girl has got ptsd

How are you supposed to
Get to know me?
If conversations are one-sided

I must be the only one interested
And what you said
were just words
that your actions contradict

Your sweet–sweet words
Enchanting me
Until I see the pattern of your behavior

I'd rather be alone
Shit, I'd rather talk to myself
At least I'm interesting

So don't text me
Wyd?
U up?

That shit is for the birds
Ask me about my research
Or things that inspire me

I'm deep
Introspective
Caring and reciprocal

I don't want to be
the only one making an effort
So stop leaving me on read
Just be honest
and say you're not interested

Use your words
Be an adult
And above all
don't waste my fucking time

SOLILOQUY no. 1

I'm tired

of caring

too much

about people

who

don't care

about me

I'm tired

of checking

on people

who don't

check on me

I want

reciprocal

or nothing

FWB?

I saw you there
I was unaware
To be honest, you caught my eye
But what mattered more
Was that you intrigued my mind

Out of my comfort zone
I reached out
It wasn't the right time
I put you out of my thoughts

I stayed away but,
the universe pulled us together
I was so confused
If you were taken or if it was a ruse

Your smile, your laugh
Confidence exudes
You are a star
And light up the room

I never expected to see you again
Yet there you were
Every time I turned my head
You, your smile, your presence

The warmth you ooze
I lose myself in you
Your arms protect me,
and shield me like never before

When we kiss
The world disappears
And are the only ones in the room
Time does not exist

All I need is you
I know you will always have my back
And will forever be my home
You are everything I want in a partner
But we are nothing more than
Friends with benefits

"NAKED AND AFRAID"

I feel so bad because I digressed and operated out of a place of lack... and I acted illogically.

I should have trusted ███████ sooner. I feel horrible because this asshole used me and lied to me. I feel violated, and worse because I can't tell ███████ because it would hurt him.

I didn't know if we were exclusive though I wanted to be... I was afraid of trusting him and falling in love. Now that I realize all of this, it might be too late.

He might not want to talk to me because I'm still married... technically, but I'm sure that I told him? I feel very sad, and I want nothing more but to hug him... but I'm not sure if I'm going to be able to.

I am also stressed and overwhelmed and I need love and support right now, but I don't feel like I fully have it. I still want someone who will hold me at night at least most of them... but I don't think that will ever be ███████ because he lives with family, and said he won't move in with me.

As much as he feels like home, I don't think he'll ever be my home. I think the damage is done. At this point I don't want to date anyone else and I'm over the dating apps. It just hard to weed through people and trust.

CONNECTION

When I think about you
I can feel the stars
I feel a deep magnetism
To you
Visceral
In my bones
But beyond them too
The center of-you-the-universe
In you, in me, in us
A deep trust that we both
Mistrust
So we deny
And we fight
We play petty games
To spite
Matching wit and attitude
You're rude, but I am too
Same sense of humor
Dirty and fun
You complement me well
But what I love
Are the things that
We share in common
Exhilarated and faded
Jaded and never dated
Just linked
And we both knew
That this is what we're going to do
Me & you

self———

—— reflection

A GIRL FROM GARY

I guess you can say it was always in me. I guess you could say this the true me.

A girl from Gary, take the girl up out the hood. Can't take the hood out of me. I'll always be a girl from Gary.

I find it hard to relate. Ain't none of y'all been through the shit. I went through

Gary had me on the floor.

Surrounded by my blood.

Dragged me by my hair.

Caged bird I broke free.

Resilient me, I became who I'm meant to be.

They got Meek askin' what's free? I tell you what, it's me. I'm free. Liberated completely.

I keep my circle,
like I keep my pussy,
tight. Scorpio Moon, don't
trust nobody.

Get in my face we might fight. Step to me step to me. Bitch you don't know me.

You gonna make me turn me back into the old me.

SEE ME

I want to be seen
        be known
            loved
                accepted
For who I am
        not despite of
        who I am
I want to be exactly what someone
      wants
      and
           needs
              and can't live without
I don't want to be
     too much
        or feel like I'm not enough
I want to be the person
     that they've
        been waiting for
           their entire life
II want to be their perfect match

SURVIVAL MODE

Inhale
Exhale

Breathing
keeps me alive

To live
to keep going

Remember
to breathe

UNTITLED no. 6

I want that love that people write songs about

I want you to choose me everyday

And I will be there for you, no question

My love and devotion is deeper than the ocean

But it's never been reciprocated

I just want someone to hold me

And love on me every night

Kiss me on the forehead when we part

And hug me like you're never letting go

I want something real and lasting

I want something that feels good

I want to feel safe and comfortable

And damn, I want our love to be easy

SOMETHING DIFFERENT

I want to be loved

I want to be wanted

And needed

And cared for

And cherished

Desired

Happy

I'm tired of being alone

Used, hurt

Sad

WISHING ON A STAR

Love,

Be with me

Hold me

Grow with me

I need you to be patient

While I unlearn how I've been loved

In order to receive and accept

The love I deserve

Your love

...ABOUT ME

My ass
It jiggles and shakes

My hips
The curve from my waist

My luscious lips
Little hands and cute feet

My eyes
Hazel and deep

My roundness
And soft edges

My light touch
And voluptuous voice

All of this woman
Unmistakably

Behind the flouncy hair
And hazel eyes
Under he soft and tender curves

Lies a remarkable mind
With thoughts so vast
So precise

She's very wise
Ahead of her time

She's so much
And requires a sensual touch

Because not everyone can handle
This much woman

SOMETIMES

Sometimes
I feel like
I'm never going to be loved
or have a partner
or be happy

Sometimes
It feels like
I was made to be alone
Like I was made to suffer
Like I can only exist in pain

Sometimes
I wish my life were a nightmare
That I could wake up from
Not my reality so I can escape

Sometimes
I don't want to live
I don't want to even try to
I just want to give up

Sometimes
I'm so down
I can't even see a way up
or even keep my feet moving

Sometimes
I wish my memories
Weren't my own
That I had amnesia
I wish I could forget it all

But I'm haunted
And the weight of the trauma
Is heavy and burdensome
And the only way to describe it is
"too much"

SANDRA CISNEROS

It was *Hips*
I fell in love with poetry

The song the girls sing
In *The House on Mango Street*

Esperanza, she wanted hips
I had them

In the song asking for hips
Something I possessed

Representation
Desire, idolized

Of Me
I saw myself

I never wanted
to be the woman in the window

Smoking and waiting
Dreaming of being free

I wanted to be the Mami
That worked

Now, I am
Representation matters

Reflected in words
A description that describes me

Sandra Cisneros, I just hope I can
have the same impact on women
that you had on me.

HAVE YOU EVER BEEN SO LONELY?

It hurts

Everything hurts

Everything is sad

Your heart longs

It feels like you can't go on

Waiting for someone

Wanting a connection

Needing to be held

But it never comes

You beckon and cry

Cry and cry

Beg and plead

For someone to

Hold me please

Kiss me

Love me

Need me

Want me

But instead it's just you

In a big empty bed

Hugging a pillow

Wishing it could hug back

Love back

Kiss back

But it's a pillow

It has no heart

And as much as you long and wait

You want to turn to ice

But you can't

Because somewhere

Out there

Someone is your person

So you cling to hope

TRUTH IS...

Truth is
I'm hurt
I'm always hurting
I'm so hurt that I don't know
What it's like to be not hurt

Truth is
I want to be loved
I want to love
I want to love so bad it hurts
But I don't know how to love
Because I've never been loved
And I've never been in love
That doesn't hurt

Truth is
Love isn't supposed to hurt
Love is supposed to be easy
It's supposed to feel good
It's supposed to be happy and filled with laughter

Truth is
I don't know how to do that
I don't know how to relax
How to not be suspicious
Or pessimistic
How to not be on alert
Because I've been hurt

Truth is
I'm tired of not trusting
I'm tired of running
Tired of trying to figure out
How someone is gonna hurt me before they do
So I push them away
Tired of crying
Because I'm lonely
Because my bed is too big
And I feel empty

Truth is
I don't know how to let go
Or how to trust
Because I've always had to
Have my own back
I don't know what it even feels like f
Or someone to have mine

Truth is
I want to open up
But vulnerability is scary
But the idea of getting hurt again is terrifying
So I push away, seclude, run away, and self-sabotage
Because I don't want to feel that hurt again

Truth is
I think that when I'm alone at night
And I'm reaching for someone
And no one is there
That's the worst hurt
And I say I don't care
But the truth is I do

PUSH

I push people away

But I really want them to stay

I just don't know

How not to be paranoid and anxious

Or how to trust and be unafraid

Trauma gets the best of me every time

And I, push. Push. Push.

Until nobody's left

Just me.

Still pushing on

But wishing

Hoping

That I wasn't alone

And that I didn't push them away

JUST ME.

Never enough but also too much?

How can I be both?

I'm just myself

An extraordinary woman

I am everything

Beautiful, smart, sexy, cool

Resilient, brave, whole

PRAY A LITTLE PRAYER

I've never had someone
Who just really cares about me
And takes care of me.

I've always had to have a plan b.
As I prepare for the worst.
All the pressure on me.

I want to be with someone
who cares for me,
and I don't just have myself to fall back on.

I want to be supported
and know someone is going to catch me if I fall.

I don't want to be the girl jumping off her bike
because she lost her balance
and doesn't want to get hurt as she's falling.

I want to fall into my person's arms.
I want to be held and feel safe and protected.
I've never had that before.

I think it'll feel good to rest
and let my guard down
finally.

JUST RIGHT

I am sweet

Like honeydew

Not overly sweet

But subtle

Understated

Mildly so

Prefect to cool the heat

Calm

Friendly

Approachable

Like honeydew

I AM

beautiful

deserving

strong

loved

whole

abundant

YO SOY

bonito

meritorio

fuerte

amado

entero

abundante

LESSONS

As I heal and learn patience
I must remember that delayed
It does not mean denied

Learning to be patient is
Releasing the expectation of time
Time doesn't work through expectations

Time is divine
It has its own plan
Releasing expectations is having faith

Faith that everything for me
Is on it's way to me
In it's own time

Don't give up
Don't get sad
Don't write it off

I WONDER WHY

Any time I feel rejected

I start thinking I don't deserve to be happy

And that no one wants me

It'll go as far as questioning why I'm alive

I haven't had suicidal thoughts in a very long time

I don't want to die or kill myself

But I question why I'm alive

Like why did I go through everything

I went through to ultimately end up alone

It's a constant did I deserve that

Why doesn't anyone see me for who I am?

UNTITLED no. 7

I know I deserve to be happy

Deserve to be loved

It hurts to open up

It hurts that I'm different

And don't have a normal brain

I have a trauma brain

I want to connect and bond

But how?

I've only known abuse

I want someone to hold me

SHE IS ME

So much more than a pretty face,
She's got style, grace,
and a mind as bright as a star

She is a star
You'd be lucky to find yourself
Around her shine
She is brilliant and
lights up a room with her smile

She wants to help because she cares
Because she's been through struggle
And survived

She shares her knowledge
To build up
the tight circle of friends around her

She is beautiful but her mind is the prize
She learns and grows through reflection
Her thoughts are deep like her feelings

She will make your knees weak
with her wit and intuition
Her intensity, and prowess

She's broken hearts
but has also been broken
Yet she survived, and is beginning to thrive

UNTITLED no. 8

I am so grateful for the love I have in my life

I am so lucky

To receive and to give

Reciprocity

PUSHING THROUGH

I crave the things I'm scared of
I don't know how to be in healthy relationships
I always had people putting me down
Or using me or abusing me

It's hard for me to think or even come to terms that people like me
I want a healthy and happy marriage and a close extended family
relationship and babies damn I want babies

I want a house with a big yard and porch and a puppy to play with
I want to be comfortable enough to consistently work out and not fear
unwanted attention or assault/rape

I want to have a partner who knows me and I don't have to say or
vocalize my pain when I'm triggered or have a flashback

I want a partner who is kind and patient and accepting of me, the way
I am but wants to grow with me and see me heal

I don't want to hurt anymore and I don't want to want anymore

This is mine, I will have it - I know I deserve all these things

I am worthy of love
I am desirable
I am beautiful
I am smart
I am good enough

UNTITLED no. 9

I have been thinking about resilience a lot lately.

It's safe to say, I have it in my bones.

REFLECTED

Sometimes I look in the mirror
> and this is who I see staring back at me.

Physical scars faded,
> but the mental and emotional scars are still there.

Loving myself, overcoming insecurities,
> and believing in myself comes from within.

You don't see what I see.
> I know I am more than my scars,
> I know I am more than my trauma,
>> but I still see her—

>>> my lowest point.

>> My rock bottom—
>>> and it's hard to look away.

Her eyes are piercing and swollen,
> her lips are busted and bruised,
>> and her nose is held together by stitches.

Seventy-two stitches, to be exact.

AFTERNOON DELIGHT

I listen to the silence.

I feel the warmth of the sun

Across my face.

I take a deep breath in

And I breath it out.

The rhythm of life.

The purrs of my cat.

The sound of a car driving by.

Water flowing somewhere.

A bird chirping.

My own heartbeat

Reminds me I'm alive.

Another day to be grateful.

Another day to smile.

Another chance to give

And receive love.

UNTITLED no. 10

I'm beautiful because of
the things I've survived

They changed me,
refined me, and transformed me

Because of pain,
I know happiness

Because of struggling,
I know triumph

Because of sadness,
I know love

Because of hurt,
I know pleasure

Because I once settled,
I know what I deserve

I am not the same person I once was,
and because of that
I know what I want and need

I am better
and therefore deserve better

My soul calls out to my partner,
I can't wait to be with you

WHAT I NEED

I am love
It pours out of me
I give it freely
My heart aches
Because I yearn to feel love
I just want to nurture and help
My future partner grow
That is love
I want to be held at night
And hugged when I see you
The gentle touch of moving my hair
so you can see my face
Your arm around me while we watch tv
Or you laying with your head on my lap
Your hands rubbing my leg
My head on your chest
Holding hands
Rubbing feet
This is love to me
I need the love of being touched
I need the love of quality time and conversation
I've been without them for so long
I yearn for love
It hurts me so much
I need human connection

DREAMING OF YOU

I need and want someone in my life
That needs and wants me in theirs.

That cares about me and is going to check on me.
That wants to hear about my day and tells me about theirs.

That looks forward to cuddling
And holding each other at the end of the day.

That wakes up smiling at me, fucks me good and smacks me on the
ass/ kisses me on the cheek when telling me to have a good day.

Someone who doesn't need to talk to me all day
But could if they (and myself) had the time.

Someone who loves me with their whole self
And someone who I can love with all of me.

Someone who wants to share
Their life, bed, and have babies (or adopt) with me.

Someone who shows me they want me.
So I never have to wonder or guess.

Send me that person,
Send me my partner.

It hurts not to have them in my life yet,
I know I deserve their love and they deserve mine.

ICE COLD

Call me ice, ice, baby
Bitch, I don't mean baby

I mean ice
I'm not nice

I'm a cold ass bitch
I'll break your heart

Don't act like I didn't
Tell you that from the start

He say he love me
But everybody love me

Love my body
Love my booty

Dudes Telling me "besame cutie"
Bitches hatin' so I say "sue me"

They think I want they man
Bitch I don't want yo man

Too many boys
actin' like they grown

I look down from my throne
HBIC — pussy on a pedestal

Sliding in my DM's
Telling me I'm beautiful
Acting really pitiful

Can't go nowhere
Without hearing "goddamn"
I guess he saw my ass

I just keep it moving
Everybody love me

But I ain't got time
For anyone except me

Quit catching feelings
They ready and willin'

My heart cold like hielo
I don't need you

I'm broken and
I'll only break you

And I'll just make you cry

WHAT I WANT

Be obsessed with me
Talk to me consistently
Look at me adoringly
Crave my body
Miss my lips
When they part from yours

Know every freckle and birthmark on my body
Ones that I don't even know are there
Hold my hand and rub my thumb
Put your head on my chest

Be my safe space and be mine
Make me feel secure
Protect me physically
Create space for me
Emotionally support me

Love on me
And never let me go

CAN I LOVE?

What is love?
Why can't I love?
Going back and forth in my head
Trying to figure out
What and why and how

I know I want it
I don't know if I've been loved
I don't know if I've ever been in love
Fairy tales seem far off from reality

Happy endings...
Are people really happy?
I guess I don't understand love
How can I?

I only know trauma, abuse, and pain
Been so broken and hurt
Abandoned
Ice cold and my guard up

Can't let anyone in
I don't want to hurt again
Deep wounds
Ones that won't scab or scar

Tears flow, constantly
Always alone
How can I not be?
Do it myself
Only I got me

I know this comes from pain
My broken places
The hidden parts
Deep inside

The things I don't talk about
What I can't share
Opening up is reopening my wounds
Not fully healed
Will I ever be?

Will I ever know what it feels like to be safe?
To be held, protected, and loved?
I don't even know what would feel like?

Can I love?
Can I be loved?
Can I let myself be loved?

RUNAWAY

Runaway.
The first time I was 13.
I ran away from pain and
abuse, from my family.

They didn't build me up.
They tore me down.
They were supposed to love
and protect me. I was beaten
physically, ripped apart
verbally, and my emotions
eradicated

The second time, I was on a
plane to California.
I promised that I'd never look
back.

But, I was so low.
I couldn't see a way out.
I was stuck.
Repeating.
Replaying.

Trying so hard to escape,
but I kept being pulled into
the trauma. I knew what
I was living, wasn't worth
living. I wanted to be dead.

I made rash decisions.
Eloped.
And the next time I ran away,
was in my mind.
Hope was how I fled.

Hoping for better. Dreaming
of peace and happiness.
Wishing for love, needing
respect...
Reciprocity...
Loyalty and persistence.

I still run, but not away.
I run towards happiness,
and joy, and love, and
stability.

HAD TO SURVIVE

Had to survive
Had to survive
Glad I'm alive
Glad I'm alive

Bitch you don't know me
Try to step to me
You don't want none
You don't want none

Stole yo man?
Look at this ass
Not just a pretty face
Had to survive

Fighting everyday
Like it's my last
Had to grow up way too fast
But I survived

Bitch I'm alive
Doing me
Getting money for my seed
I got my back

You don't want none
Ain't got shit to lose
Fix your face
I'll dismantle you

You ain't heard about me?
Yeah, I stole yo man
I got book smarts and street
smarts
Get outta' my face

I'm that ride or die
My pussy's on a pedestal
Bow down bitch
You ain't on my level

I am everything
He's mine now
You don't want none
Step to me

See what happens
Had to survive
Had to survive
Glad I'm alive

CON MIS LABIOS

With these lips

I speak truth

And have conviction

They hold power

To share stories

With a wide smile

They bear an unseen scar

An insecurity

But, I am reclaiming my power

sexuality ———

—reflection

JUST LIKE A DRUG

That's how I feel

YOU are the best drug

and the worst

YOU make me feel everything

but **YOU** take the pain away

Touch me

Rub me

Kiss me

Lick me

Fuck me

when the world is quiet

and asleep

I just want to be near **YOU**

to feel good

YOU make me feel so good

Hold me

close

and never let me go

PHYSICAL TOUCH

Cuddles are all I need
The act of touching fills me up
Hold my hand
Let me rest my head on your shoulder
Kiss me on the forehead
I'll kiss you on your cheek
Your face in my hands
Put your arm around me
Our thighs can rub as we sit next to each other close
Our feet touch in bed
My leg over yours as we unwind
I feel connected when we cuddle
It fills my cup with love
Your love
I need it, I crave it
Love me, touch me, feel me as I feel you

ELECTRICITY

The feeling
Of your breath
on my neck
Taking me in
Feeling warm
Exhale into my inhale
Open mouths
Lips pressed
Teeth touching
Tongues licking
Intensely
Passionately
Kissing each other
Like it was The difference
between life and death
When we are together
We are alive
You are The electricity
That makes my heart beat
And without you
the greatest Despair lingers
and the hope of death Lurks

OOOOOOO...

The way you hold me
My naked body
Pressed against yours
Kissing me hard
And deep
Our hands
Pulling each other
Into ourselves
Slowly grinding
Legs intertwined
Moaning
Groaning
All in ecstasy
Oh baby
Yes please
Kiss my neck
The way you do
Ooo baby
I love you
Cum in me
Let's make a baby

IN BETWEEN THE SHEETS

Your hands
up and down—
my back and hips
on my waist
and butt.

Your lips
on my neck
my nipples
arms and shoulders
down my stomach
on my thighs—
in between.

Licking and tasting
along the way
making me feel
like a sexy feline—
you make me frisky.

I pull you into me
no gaps or spaces
between us—
we melt into each other.

The moans and groans—
all the sounds of ecstasy
nothing and no one else exists
when we are together.

Intense, lustful, passionate
intimate—
kissing, hugging, loving
each other—
soaking it all in.

Time stopping—
earth shattering—
breathing fresh air
into me.

I was starting to drown
treading water too long—
looking and searching
for the love of my life.

And there you are—
our foreheads pressed together
becoming one
we already are—
because you are my home.

THUNDER

It was back when
I was just tryin' to get a tip
                        at subway
She walked in
And I could barely speak
I had to take her order
I don't remember what she ordered
                        just that she was wearing
                        white jeans and a yellow tank top
Her thighs
Hips and cute butt
Her face was beautiful, too
But as I stood making her sandwich
Being shy and avoiding her eye
Just her hips and thighs were in my view
I never understood the fascination of white jeans before
But I did in that moment
Her jeans were a little see through
I could see her bright pink thong
                                and I liked it
I could see her cute pedicured toes and petite feet
But I never made eye contact
But she is forever etched in my mind
Because that was the day
                        I knew
                        without a doubt
                        that I was gayyyyyyyyy
I wasn't drunk or high
I didn't know anything about her
And yet I wanted her to smother me with her thunder thighs

COMING OUT

He said, "I knew it!"

Exclaiming this

after I said, "I'm not straight."

I exhaled

and let out the breath

that I was holding

Seven years

After realizing my truth

While working at Subway

In a loveless marriage

Closeted

And scared to come out

Hiding my truth

Gasping for air

To breathe, to live

Now authentically, me.

Love me or hate me

Or let me be

Liberated

Free to love

Free to feel love

To express my love

With her, or him, or they

Or show myself the best love

I love myself

That's why I walked away

That's the reason I said no

I have to live with myself

I'm not gonna go another day

Not living my truth

I'm happy now, confident, whole

I'm home now, I am home

Home is in me, my body

OTHER

Why am I hyper-sexualized?
Who will see me for who I am and want me?
I've been hurt too much
I've been through too much
I want someone to hold me
I want someone to love me
To support me
God damn I'd give them everything I can
All of me
If they see all of me—why am I still hyper-sexualized?
Who will see me for who I am and want me?
I've been hurt too much
I've been through too much
I want someone to hold me
I want someone to love me
To support me
God damn I'd give them everything I can
All of me
If they see all of me

JERK IT

You wanted pictures of my lips
You had a thing with lips
You jerked it to my lips

My curves my curves
You dreamt about my curves
You jerked it to my curves

Breast and nipples
Lacy bra
You jerked it to the thought

My pretty feet
You told me you want them
You jerked it thinking bout me

Tell me about my eyes
What did you say about them
Keep em open when you're inside
Jerk it to my eyes

Lick lick lick
All around my clit
Kiss it baby
You wish wish wish
Just jerk it baby
To my clit

Pretty pussy
Juicy, fat, and tight
Wish you could fill me up

Shake shake shake
Jiggle them cakes
Can't keep your load
Jerking to my cakes

Watch me twerk
The way my ass shakes
When I twerk twerk twerk
And you jerk jerk jerk

Late night FaceTime
Telling me you want me
Jerking to my face

Say you like my voice
Makes you feel so good
Listening to my voice
Telling me you want to
Jerk it to my voice

Love the way you want me
But you know you can't have me
So you just jerk it to the thought of me
I'm just your fantasy

SEX

My sex, our sex…
I'm told I'm good at it.

Is it me?
Or is it you?
Idolizing my body

Fetishizing my waist to hip ratio
Dehumanizing my ass

Telling me "you got good hair"
But what the fuck is good hair?!

Damn near worshiping me
While putting down my
Melanated sisters

But oh, my sex is good?
I had to stop faking it

You don't bring me pleasure
Tolerating you, at best

I just lay there
And you go ooohhh

Best you ever had
But boo you're forgettable

Sex for me isn't just physical
It's metaphysical

Soul bonds, intellectual trysts
The touch, your fingertips

I don't want men
who just fetishize me
I want reciprocity and peace

Sex with men is
good for them
bad for me

But…with women
It's titillating, slow, mental, erotic,
emotional, intimate … warm,
sex with women is life.

self————

transformation

TAKING FLIGHT

I think about that flight
Every time I get on a plane
The one where I left
And I did not look back
My first solo trip
To get away
Was I running?

Escaping
Making a new life
Going through what I did
Growing through it
Oversized bag fees
What did I need to bring
With me to start over?

How much of my old life did I need?
The next solo flight would be to get away
From the life I was stuck in
Loveless marriage
Overworked, overwhelmed
Tired, underpaid
Drowning working mom

Absent partner
He took up space
Breathing all the oxygen
Not leaving enough
So that I could
Catch my breath
Continuously under water

He took everything I had
Threw it out the window
Until I couldn't take it anymore
I had to take more flights
Solo flights
An independent woman emerged
Only dependent on herself

And the solo trips continued
A drive here or there
Drove across the country
Twice
Alone
Strong woman
Fearless woman
Taking flight
Taking off

A PLACE CALLED HOME

I used to search,
for a place called home.

It wasn't in my past, or
present but maybe it'd be in
my future? Was it the family
I had? The one I never had?
Always wanted? What did
it look like? Where was it?
Here? There? Anywhere?
Everywhere? Nowhere?

I searched high and low.
Across the country. On the
Internet. At the bottom of
bottles In faces and places I
didn't know. In my bed and
others'.

But I left. I ran away. Again
and again searching. But
alas I'm a crab. A Cancer,
I burrow. I run, hide and

search. For a home, to
replace the old one. The one
I outgrew. Because home
isn't a shelter, or certain
people, blood or not.

Home is me. I am my own
home. My home is my body.
And I live in my body. I am
home wherever I am.

Wherever I run or hide. My
shell, my exterior, my armor,
it protects me. A part of
me. It might look different
sometimes. A little broken,
cracked, or shiny and
sparkly.

The exterior is only a
reflection of me. I am my
own home. Inside my body,
my mind, and soul.

BREAKING FREE

I was once contained

Encased in glass

Crack by crack

The case remained

I could not escape

This case was there

To silence me

Until the shatter

Shards and tiny pieces of glass

Everywhere

Broken

How I felt

But then I realized

I was water inside

A glass case

I could never be contained

I am free to flow

The broken case

The pain and hurt

I left behind

To live unleashed and free

ARWEN

If you want me
Come get me
I'm not chasing
I need to be chased
Pursue me
Choose me
Need me
like you need to breathe

BETTER NOW

I'm falling
not from the sky
but from
>*where you you pushed me down*
>*where you held me down*
>*at my lowest point*

I SURVIVED
I CRAWLED
I STOOD
I WALKED

Now here **I AM**
I've **OUTGROWN YOU**

You, who didn't love me
You, who put me down
So you, could feel better about yourself

Now, I'm flying
>*so far past you*
>*over you*
>*far away*

Now, I'm safe
I'm better now

SCARS

Some might call them battle wounds

Damaged, or trauma

Physical and Mental

Scars

Looking in the mirror is triggering

I see a glaring scar

How can someone call me beautiful?

Unnoticed by others

But it's all I see sometimes

The physical scars are nothing compared

To the deep emotional lesions in my mind

They are connected by the trauma

Painful memories

Lack of memories

Jumbled thoughts, confusion

Panic, anxiety

Lack of sleep

They take me up and down

And isolate, I can't breathe

I'm drowned in the trauma

These scars are a plague on my very being

How do I heal

Can I heal

Am I broken

Am I damaged goods

Will someone want me

Why did I have to go through this

Did I deserve it

These questions constantly circle in my mind

Like a shark circling prey

Anxiety keeps attacking my hope

My anxiety, I created it

It comes from my trauma

My anxiety is only as bad as my trauma

I thought I was healed

But I just buried it all, ignored it

And the anxiety was left

Trying to protect me

But drowning me

Snuffing my breath

Freezing my heart

Putting my life on hold

Frozen in time

Scars reopening

I'm trying to heal them

UNTITLED no. 11

It's worst when I'm alone

The pain

Have you ever been so lonely

That it hurts you physically?

Your heart hurts

Your mind

Your soul

How can loneliness...

hurt your soul?

I feel it deep in my chest

Longing

Wanting

For the comfort of a warm hug

An embrace

To feel wanted

To finally know love

UNTITLED no. 12

waiting.

for.

the.

other.

shoe.

to.

drop.

because that's,

what you're used to.

but there isn't another shoe.

and you realize that excitement

really does feel like anxiety.

PAIN

In pushing yourself
There is pain

It's not just uncomfortable
It's painful too

Out of your comfort zone
Uncomfortable and Painful

Transformation happens
When you are uncomfortable

Turn the pain
Into power

Transform yourself
But transmute your pain
Into power

You will be a force
To be reckoned with

REJECTED

I've been rejected more times than I can count

It's always the same story

They don't want labels, just want to be friends, only want to have sex, they need business advice or I'm nice but...or I have a nice butt...

I'm intimidating, too smart, too pretty, too damaged, too clingy or not clingy enough

Am I rejected because I'm me?

Or because you are insecure?

All these ideas about who I am, and how I live my life and navigate the world

But you don't know how many people that were no match for me but have rejected me

You don't know the daily bullshit I go through, just to show up for myself

You don't know that my whole life, I was rejected and reduced

I used to shrink, but I healed the child within and I'm not that scared little girl anymore

Afraid to talk or show how smart, or talented and kind she is, just because she didn't want to be noticed

I've done everything I can to hide

But I was too bright of a star

People saw me anyway

NOT A PICKME

i'm not too much to love
or not enough
these are things that
people have said to me,
about me,
because they could not admit
that they could not love me

i am enough
i am not a piece or a part
i am whole

so i wait for what i deserve
i cut anyone off
that doesn't see me
that plays games
wastes my time
and that doesn't accept me

i know what i want
and what i need
and I can give in return
everything that i ask for

i can be everything
i can give space
i'm the shoulder you cry on
the one whose hugs warm your soul
and is all about pleasure in bed

i command a boardroom
but submit in the bedroom
i throw down in the kitchen
and will try to cuddle and kiss in every room

didn't i say that i am everything?
the healer, the mother, the thot, the chef,
the badass, the boss, and the best friend

there are no more pieces of me
you can't have just half or a part
it's all of me or none of me
i'm whole
and only another whole person can love me
i know that, in my soul

THIRD EYE

I've been searching for freedom
And I've finally found it

I've searched and I've longed
It wasn't where I thought it'd be

I found freedom in myself
Not in others or in things

I know why the caged bird sings
I'm the bird and my mind was the cage

Leave it all in the past
Letting it go

Growing from pain
Releasing it

Taking the lesson
No more running away

I'm moving forward
Running towards what I deserve

My mind is free
My soul sings

I can finally be me
Nothing holding me back

AFTER TRAUMA

I hate that I'm fucked up
I hate that I haven't been able to have
a healthy relationship
I hate that I want a family so bad
I hate that I get so down and negative
I hate that I'm lonely
I hate that people think differently of me
when they find out I have trauma
It's not easy to walk around like this
It's not easy to trust people
I want to trust so bad
I want to be loved so bad
It hurts so bad

Why am I so fucked up?
Why did I have to go through those things?
Why do I have to walk around life like this?
I wish I was easy to love?
I want someone who sees all of me and still wants me

WEATHERING A STORM

When I felt I was at my lowest point...
I knew there was only one place to go from there.

Up.

I've picked myself up and had my own back
more times than I'd like to admit to.

The funny thing is; that I didn't realize I was being
resilient, until I reflected after the fact.

Hope has a way of pushing you if you are resilient.
That idea that things are going to get better.
It can't rain all the time.

We weather the storm
and we come out stronger than ever.

The rain does something else to us,
it nurtures and helps us grow.

Sometimes it's painful, and you think there's no end.
But then a ray of sunshine peeks through the clouds.
A rainbow glitters the sky.
The birds begin to chirp.
And you bask in the glow of the sunshine.

There's still some time before the puddles dry up...
And it might drizzle a bit, but the worst is over, and you
being to pick up the pieces that have gone astray.

That's hope.
Pushing you along and reminding you...
it can only get better.

I WILL BREAK YOU

Has someone ever instantly fell in love with you?

Only to realize...
    that...
        they are everything...
      that you thought you wanted for years...
but ...
    you've grown so much...
        that you outgrew the idea...
            and you didn't know it...
                until you met them..
Now, I have to hurt you.
    I'm going to hurt you,
        not because you're a red flag,
            but because we're not aligned.
Because now, I want so much more.
    I started to dream up my next phase of life,
        and the person that checks all the boxes,
            of the list of thins that I used want...
                only prevents me from living my best life.
I am, single by choice,
    independent as hell,
        soon to be world traveler,
            she's successful by her own standards ,
                and a mother to one and done.
Your life doesn't go with mine,
    your plan is nice...
        but I've transcended all of the,
            traditional values and social constructs.
            I am liberated.
You are not.
    That's not to say you won't ever be,
        but I can't wait...
            for anyone...
                to get ready for me.
I need someone who is ready now,
    I need a match,
        no compromises.

PHOENIX RISING

For so much of my life I let external forces
get to me. They brought me down,
they hurt me, they oppressed me, they
suffocated me, they burned me.

I've been burning. All of these experiences
were required, they weren't pleasant or fun
and some were downright degrading.
I thought I deserved it all for some reason,
I thought life was cruel and believed
that I was worth how I was treated.

Now I am reborn. Like a phoenix I am rising
from the ash that was the past. It made me
who I am. All those external forces that I
internalized, the negativity, the pain,
the shame, the fear… it is no more.
I've been shown I'm so much more.
I have transformed. I am myself,
and I am owning every part of me.

My story makes me unique
and it breathes life into me. I have so much
to offer, I am so much - there isn't a
doubt in my mind now.

To those who burned me,
stand back - I have ignited.

future ————

———————— self

Dear Universe,

Please send me my soulmate.

Dear Soulmate,

Where are you? I need your touch, your warmth. I look forward to laughing with you and sharing joy. Hold my hand, dance with me... Be my best friend.

I need your tender love, consistent love, your grounding love. I'm ready for your kindness and your loving gaze. I need your embrace, your sweet kisses, and calming demeanor.

I want to hear your voice whisper affirmations in my ear, say my name, and tell me you love me.

I want to talk to you for hours about everything and nothing. I want to be near you. I want you to hold me, and let me feel your love.

I'm ready for you soulmate, come to me. I have so much love to give you. I'm ready to pour into you.

My heart is already yours. My body is waiting for you. My mind anticipates you. Our souls are already one... Come to me, my forever love.

Find me. I'm ready for your love.

Always & Forever,

Naomi

I FEEL

I feel so sad
So broken
So alone

I'm waiting on my soulmate
To find me
To hold me
To love me

I need you
Wherever you are
I'm ready for your love

Life has been hard without you
Without true love
It broke me down

I built myself up
To find you
I deserve you
I deserve love

I feel you out there
So close
My hand out
Please take it
And never let go

I'M HERE.

Dear Soulmate,

I await your arrival in my life. I'm here, ready for you with open arms. I'm ready to share laugh and meals, our time together... I'm ready to hold, kiss, and love one another.

I'm ready for our reciprocal love. A lasting friendship. Mutual respect and admiration. I'm ready to hold hands and hug.

I'm ready to hear about your day, everyday. I'm ready to hold you in times of pain. Smile with you in times of joy.

I await our journey together, learning and growing with you. I can't wait to see you with my son. Being a role model to him.

Having our own family and live our life together. My love, I'm waiting for you. Please make your way to me. I'm right here.

Naomi

IF I HAVE TO

I can do it alone

But...

I want a partner

I'm tired

And at times, lonely

I need help

And Love

Support

Someone to hold me,

Have my back

And hold my hand

MANIFEST

I'll keep saying it
Until it becomes my reality

I AM forever grateful
I AM grateful for the life I have
I AM grateful for the people in my life
The ones who ride for me
The ones that test me
And the ones that teach me

I AM ready to be loved as my whole self
By another whole person who is ready to love me

I AM ready to be held
And kissed, and spoiled
I AM ready to be taken care of
I AM ready to be chosen
and complimented, not completed

I AM ready for my partner
I have so much to give to you

CLINGY & NEEDY

Cuddles and sex
Neck and back rubs

Soft touches on my back
My butt getting smacked

I just want to be touched
Rubbed, loved, held

I want to feel my heart warm
From the sensation
of being in your arms

I want to feel safe
I want to feel secure

I want to feel at home
With you, in you

Hold my hand
Let me rest my head
on your chest

Feel your fingers
In my hair
On my shoulder

Kiss my forehead
Squeeze me tight

Love me
Love me
Love me

LIKE NEVER BEFORE

I'm so ready,
for love

The kind of love,
I deserve

The kind of love,
I've been waiting for

The kind of love,
I know exists

The kind of love,
that will give me a home

The kind that will last forever
The kind that makes me smile

The kind that holds me
And sees me

I'm ready to be loved
like never before

SOUL READY

I am ready
My soul is ready
Ready to find you

Stop looking
I'm here
Dear soulmate

Let me look in your eyes
Let me feel your soft lips on my skin
Hold me and never let me go

We are found
We are one
We are love

And we are trust,
And loyalty and
All good things

Take my hand
We'll do this together
Side by side

MAGNETIC

I dream of the day
that I can be with you.

Intertwined,
introspective,
and intimate.

Lovingly
hold me.
Pull me in.

My partner,
my love,
my best friend.

I FEEL SO FREE

Fucking—just look at me
I'm rhyming in the mirror
Like Issa Dee

It's like—I could
or—I would, but really
Should—I

Wonder why—you don't cry
or should—I just
Pack my feelings—and go

SINCE YOU'VE BEEN GONE

I have so much more energy

And I have so much more love to give to the
other people that matter in my life

Friends,
who have been there for me
People who are family

Just because they love
how I love their family

That was the same way
that I loved you

I gave it all to you
and that's on me
not to save any for myself

But damn, if you cared
Why did you take it all

How come
you never said it was too much

Because the truth is
you wanted my love

And all it came with
Except for me,
and the loving me back part

I was so open
and honest and clear
I thought I was

But somehow
you got confused
or maybe misconstrued

My therapist said
Maybe she's hurting too?

I said I don't know,
she acts like she hates me

None of it matters anymore
though—because
we aren't friends

You made that very clear
So to me, that means
it was all fake

You wanted to paint this picture perfect
portrait of a family

And I don't fit in it
Nor does my child

Maybe it's by choice
But maybe it's by design

I like to keep people in my life
Because I've lost so many

I've never broke up with a friend before
It does hurt more than
breaking up with someone you were dating

I have questioned my life
All my choices
And I wonder why I ignored the red flags?

You have a pile of discarded best friends
At least, I find myself in good company

You got me twisted
You contradict yourself
You don't know what you want

You are an air droplet in the wind
changing your direction
with every push and pull
That force provides

At least rain and snow
eventually make it to the ground
and leaves do too

But water droplets evaporate
The particles separate
From the constant back and forth

The inconsistency
And you see me
In the distance

Because I am a River
I am my own force

And I tried to give you
As much as I could

To guide you and teach you
But you didn't want it

I was trying to give you
the lessons without the pain

Because I've been there
I spent years to get to where I am now

Yes, I'm stable now
Yes, I needed and accepted help

But that was a lesson
I learned the hard way

If I was quick to accept help,
I would have learned the lesson
I learned in 8 years in only 1
That's something I was humbled by

You let your pride and your insecurity
Get the best of you

Self sabotage
I know it well

You didn't want to hear a word of what I said
You wanted or expected it to be easy
Because I did it

And low key you've always judged me by my
weight - it was in the questions about what
I eat and why I don't go to the gym oh and
buying me a maternity shirt and saying we
need to eat healthier

You'll probably say I had no idea and
pretend to be ditzy but you're not

I know how smart you are
I've seen how manipulative you can be

I've seen you on your best day
and your worst

And I held your hand - literally and
figuratively so what the absolute fuck!?

It's not okay, and it won't ever be
And that's because I was willing to forgive

But you shut it down
I just wanted to you to help yourself

You have to believe you can do hard things

Here I am still thinking about you,
thinking about ways you could help yourself
I hope that you learn to love yourself

And practice what you preach
And be your own best friend

You don't need anything from anyone
You only think you do

DARE TO

I learned to say, "it's getting there"
That's my way of saying a work in progress

That's my way to acknowledge progress
but also that the work isn't done yet

It's the in between
The gray, the mess

I like this abstract, messiness
the non-linear

Healing, unlearning
Learning, and healing

There's no concrete timeline,
everyone is different

Different end goals, starting points,
difficulty levels, experience

You get the picture
Make room for creative destruction

Hold space to become
undone

Allow yourself to unravel
Be free

To dream, of liberation

"MOM. YOU CAN'T RUSH TIME."

Things don't happen
when I want them to.

They happen when
they are supposed to.

That is divine.

That is cosmic.

And like my Virgo son said;

"You can't rush time."

Naomi Marie is, has been, and will always be "A girl from Gary". Naomi has been making a name for herself as, "Chingona Healer" a name that encompasses aspects of Naomi's radical change-maker mindset and her deeply intuitive and spiritual gifts. To be Chingona, means to be an independent, strong, bold Latina—part of a generation reclaiming the word that was once used to put down Latinas for being unapologetically themselves. For more synonyms see: La Jefa. To be a healer is to be a bruja, intuitive and deeply spiritual—all titles Naomi wears proudly.

As Chingona Healer and A girl from Gary, Naomi uses spiritual wisdom and traditional knowledge to help cultivate interpersonal growth through inspiration and storytelling. Teaching others by speaking about her transformative journey.

Currently, Naomi lives in Los Angeles, California with her son. She is happily divorced, disentangled, and living her best life. Naomi holds a Bachelor's degree in Graphic Design as well as a Master's degree in Social Innovation. She hopes to lead change towards equity using design and research as tools for change making.

Follow Naomi on Instagram and Facebook @Chingona.healer
Don't forget to check out her shop at ChingonaHealer.com

Printed in Great Britain
by Amazon

86321022R00122